Four Oceans

Four Oceans

Toby Davidson

PUNCHER & WATTMANN

First published in 2020
Published by Puncher and Wattmann
PO Box 279
Waratah NSW 2298

http://www.puncherandwattmann.com
puncherandwattmann@bigpond.com

NATIONAL
LIBRARY
OF AUSTRALIA

A catalogue entry for this book is available from the National Library of Australia.

ISBN   9781925780734

Cover design by Miranda Douglas
Typesetting by Morgan Arnett
Printed by Lightning Source International

Contents

Turn Back

You have come in the least
of your free time
to here,

for no fit reason and against
the predominantly
unconscious

wishes of reasonable people.
They would have
you decide

what's the point of it, surely
it pays to err on
the side

of prose. Don't fall through
the cracks in lines
from a friend,

you won't know what's in
them. Worse yet,
you'll get on.

Absorb only under strict
medical care,
or that

of your innermost homeland
minister, or find
you once

had a storied future, then
things were in
the wind.

You were seen with poetry,
jaundiced, spare.
Secondhand

even, a neighbour flared.
Settlers' and soldiers'
ghosts

are no excuse. They'll
launch into
anything.

Indian Pacific

From the waters of the Western sea
To the Eastern ocean sand,
The Indian Pacific spans the land.
Oh, the Indian Pacific spans the land.
      Joy McKean, 'Indian Pacific', performed by Slim Dusty

your rails
your thin
your thin paper wings
get up in your sun
fly high
dangling
dangling
your window shattered in the wind
      Underworld, 'Juanita: Kiteless'

Into the bracing cloudless distance
two lines run as one, shake scales of rust
from an East Perth Station footbridge,
down where the Indian Pacific thrums,
its sand-scoured doors flung open, filling.
Eight hundred metres to a brawny engine
the first of four-point-three thousand ks
to Sydney, best part of three sleeps away.

The seats inside are tired, red-ribbed,
two to a row, with grey headrests, arms.
Our cabin speaker cracks to life, hectors
families, riff-raff, stuff: *Ensure visitors
have left the carriages. Secure exit doors.*
Blown kisses sense a threshold closing;
passage to now a rehearsal for this.

I've walked the same roads late enough.
I've tasted the sea since before I could say.
I'll miss my crew. I've one friend East.
Got everything? Now it's down to just this:
a whirling door, pledges to call,
doona, snacks, an old backpack of clothes.
Mum, Dad relieved by my iron deliverer.

I'm in 'Red Kangaroo', a non-sleeper in three states, third row right,
behind a family from Zimbabwe.   Trans-Australian motion rouses
imperceptibly at first: a crank release, low buzz and we're off

in figment-ligament-firmament-line, the undergroan intact, intact.
    We pick up pace over diesel-stained sand, weeds bejewelled
with last night's rain, wobbling pools like the trails of divers.

Maylands, Bayswater, Bassendean pass, a Midland stop—then out!
My dual window rattles its dice of stiff, iridescent green flies; three
madcap friends to go the distance, half their luck (now they're out of it).

    Gutted utes of last-chance suburbs, rivers of glass through a hole
in asbestos, whooshing billboards that can't win us back, then vineyards,
boys nursing BMX bikes under tinny rings of a vacant crossing

and, over the seat, obsidian eyes. *Hi, I'm Elijah. That's my brother.*
He's four. He's shy. Guess what? I'm gonna be an actor. The best.
What you writing? Hey, you listening? Mum, I'm not, I'm just—bye!

Jolting on with white tea, coffee, thin sachets of tourist history
(typhoid, gold and all that money) served to thirty carriages.
We fought the land and won the flag. Died to thrive now.

End recording. Brief orchestral air.   Points of interest fade
to a country song (upbeat Slim, as they lay it on thick): *From coast
to coast by night and day, hear the clickin' of the wheels* ...

The Indian Pacific tacks up trenches where they made the cut
through blackened granite, sick-green lichen, grass trees,
frenzying bone-dry canopies; shadow a film reel snagged on

my cell (quick wave to my flickering opposite). A tipping point
hurls blood to the front and we kink to the floor of the Avon Valley.
Relief sets in as axles sigh, thrust assumes an even clip

of three point three thousand horsepower clattering. I doze,
headphoned, to lush electronica: Sasha's San Francisco set
with Narcotik's 'Platform', its respiratory rain effect muffling

cabin elders, parlour games to ignore dying farms, chimneyed altars
to a burning land. Skeletons of industry flake around a few terse gums.
Old salts chide GM canola as beats thunder up into calcium.

I rove the cars, each flying can of numb and scowling air, shuffling
like a hospital patient, party to a malevolent gravity. Gold, Red Kangaroo
classes mix in the 50s-themed diner car to jags of dashing scrub.

Gotta do it, I s'pose, see something … Can't sleep in a seat, rather
pass out pissed in the bloody smokers' caboose … Ay, can one-a-youse
buy us a pie? Pay ya in Adelaide, serious. Girls make moustaches

of sun-tipped plaits, writhe about, fall bored.   Somewhere out past
Kellerberrin, fences lose their grip, become entangled in hypotheses
stretched to a state beyond dimensions: mercy stumped for answers,

circumspect as the last post, a last bird's bugle racking brassy glyphs
into an ambient topsand.   Along an ocean floor now—to surface
is to disappear completely like oar blades of cloud retracted at a whim.

That eerie pipeline disinters itself once more from the salmon wastes.
The cabin speaker reads our minds: *Five hundred and sixty kilometres,
supplying residents with their most prized commodity—after gold—water!*

A wonder of its age. C.Y O'Connor, 'crocodile imposter' in the press, state
engineer to the last of his note: 'Put the wingwalls to Helena Weir at once—'
penned above, 'my brain is suffering ... I have lost control of my thoughts.'

Now we all see why and lounge to Michael Bolton in the dining car.
Port side, a small brown hovering hawk. Starboard, gangly rain.
    A bluebottle zapped me in a lick of water by the sculpture where

he shot himself, in surf that now bears his name. Half-spun, even wheeling
back, he caught the Mouth, Point Walter Reef, Helena and Mundaring:
cursed by black and white unalike, two horses by him, flaring.

    Pink and greys erupt from silos, arc towards beleaguered powerlines,
catch each wince of the faltering sun. The pipe resists its concrete cradles,
run-off damage, clots of earth. Three hours to Kal, then open desert.

Wetlands, crimson termite mounds surprise (one Rodin's 'Thinker', wait!)
    First day done, the lines turn in. A floating stasis tricks the mind.
Pale guests arise, stare into us til phantom branches are the only given.

We grind, stammer into Kalgoorlie,
'The Queen of the Golden Mile'.
A starlit royal blue trails over

silent brick and stone
from Hay Street Toyworld
round to the neon stables.

'YES WE ARE OPEN,
Credit Card, EFTPOS'.
Waspish pink at the edge

of the world a sight, not a scene,
for our gog-eyed band,
we aim for the high end

by the clocktower,
undeadening legs up the fateful drag
built to turn four horses round.

At The Exchange,
get blasted as the past is!
A gnome-like local tugs my sleeve:

That's the Gypsy Jokers' corner.
Standin's all right, but don't sit there.
Skimpies are great, but mate,

head down to Langtrees.
Supermodels for a hundred-n-eighty!
Not like the fat hags in the others.

He crinkles breath-close.
An' free piss on a Monday!
     Standing hours devolve

by a barrel. Dutch, Americans,
English gab. We surprise You Am I
as we split through the band room,

casing their venue for tomorrow.
Tim: *Where you from?* The Indian
Pacific. *Happy travels, man.*

We trickle down to Old Paddy Hannan,
stuck on a rock (but he started it).
James from London hugs him, skins up,

offers him a toke. It's tough as hell all night
on a corner, ask his daughters cold.
  We roam to our loaded continuum.

Back by curfew, hunkered down, lights out, we sail blue cinema
out of town consciousness, lowering our eyes at length to pillowed pits
for the tripping adept. Two-seaters unlatch and swing into cradles—

my flickering doona, Canadian Monica, star-crossed and rocking
platonic.   Orange sparks of outer mines sprint like children
for a vintage loco. My window's flies receive star travel, roll

where only time's obscene.   *Uck, uck,* a bogan sonar to the smokers'
car squeaks and cops plenty back. If all that's ahead is a rip in the dark,
they'll at least blaze through it, finding the end of the line even here.

Sigmund claimed Fyodor might have cheated his falling sickness
in Siberia, punished as he was, supernatural as he was, for when
the firing squad steadied their guns, he could see a tunnel through space ...

Cold condenses in the hollow of my hands, behind the bridge
of my nose. I'm thinned to my essential show, for audience or nada—
two impassive bone-white masks, one superimposed upon the other.

A twilit homestead's flywire door taps absently against its frame.
I start as a plump old lady bursts forth, lenses flashing excitement:
'Hello! We're so glad you're here. Will you have some tea?'

This far out, refusing's inhuman. There are no nearby houses,
just an endless violet plain. The back fence is very nearly oblivion's.
Am I some kind of detective? Children's voices peal out front,

their circle by the flower-beds. The lady stoops, delights in rhymes.
I ask about her ancient car, red, suddenly apparent. She shrugs.
'You're welcome to it, I don't drive myself.' She glances down.

'Honestly, where would I go?' 'Is that why they wouldn't take
it away?' I ask with foreknowledge I cannot have (hers?).
'Better possessed than repossessed,' she murmurs. How did I get—

Flat on my back below an old hills hoist, suburban stars corralled
by asbestos. Shouts out front, tear gas, explosions, chopper blades,
molotovs burst on the street but it's not the riot squad or the TRG,

but 1950s American cops with octagonal hats versus … all of my friends?
I rush to help or fight, but a netlike warp on a bluestone driveway
holds me back til the aftermath—wind-broomed glass and ash

at first light. So walk, what else, this Albany Highway to limestone cliffs
by a turquoise bay stretched to the blinding join. An angular woman,
made of water, stands by three coral pools. She wills me close,

inclines her brow: 'Like a jewel, the mind—' but I've already plunged
inside the first, where sediment wafts like crackling snow through
greenest caverns unconcerned with breathing my manic way.

Too young, I whoop on return. All's well that ends? The woman taller.
Her face and the peacock-eyed reef brim connectedly. Cloud-high, dry,
I now see her walk. The vast butterfly symmetry of her train.

We wake to a Nullarbor moonscape's endlessness of cairns and runes.
No ignoring it ... seats reset, lairy cocoons hatch. Threadbare scrub
prompts a tenuous earthliness (even then, withdrawn).   I snatch a pen

and rub my face. Few slept well. Two hundred ks south, a pittance here,
Eyre observed 'such startling reality ... to paralyse the mind'. His lifeline,
Wylie, watching on and on.   We blast along bored and immortal sand,

catching our minds' rolling eyes in extremis. Cobalt blue high and mighty
one eighty scans a limestone offering plate which rounds on itself
for flightless crumbs, this silver speck with its pained cicada sound.

Groans of the sleepers, inward, down, reprise their joint body
language. A distant, alien tree moves with us, like a bird or car, then stops
stock-still. Commanded? Who can tell? It's all a matter of spacecraft.

One day in, few hours on the piss, sore heads at a brekky with character.
Wal and Bruce once worked the bush. Wal survived bowel cancer.
Bruce bolts down his bacon, stares mid-smack: *Geez, this is native country.*

We're nowhere near civilisation til we see a fence and some bloody sheep.
Rhino, a TPI Vietnam vet with the Southern Cross on his great blue gut,
holds court: *They want to replace my hip—and my head! When I got back,*

biked north. Lived wild. Catch your dinner each day. Touch of paradise.
Rangers roll up—two kids—see my gun. 'You in Vietnam?' goes one.
Yeah, so what? He says, 'Mate, we've three more like you round the Point.'

Matty, more duffer than ruffian, trades valium. Steve is picaresque
human tobacco, did time in Indonesia, China. *Yeah, that was stupid.*
Shanghai was the worst. Rachael, a Minnesota teacher, gleams

Did you know if you dig up the average American after nine or ten years,
their decomposition's barely set in, because of all the preservatives?
She's fervently organic now. Outside, it's ten million years young.

10am. Ex-rail camp Cook
(for PM Joe, not fishy James).
Last rites on the longest straight track.

The halfway point, population four.
Twenty dwellings on their deathbeds,
train their only shot in the arm,

airstrip down its tawny heart
where, one day, this'll end.
 Word arrives we hit some roos;

Red Kangas clank down to inspect.
How come I only see dead ones?
Trailings away hushed up by guffaws.

 Sketchy in a purple surf shirt,
sunnies, jeans and bucket hat,
I isolate—if that's a word here—

strike out past the doorless houses,
valiant golf course, children's murals,
to an 'Evacuation Point' sign.

I ask someone I don't retain
to snap me, then I'm right off.
 Tracks, objectives, fall to none.

I duck in fright at a roaring fly.
Swallows scream like F1 jets.
Disturbance wields a master tongue.

Ants troop grain by grain.
Some sand-humps off,
self-preserving Americans

shuffle back: *I thought
I lost my hearing, it's scary* …
It's so quiet, I can't take it.

Wedgetails bleed through knots
of oxygen. Every atom spans a gong.
Amplified, I'd no doubt die here,

rightly, of imperishable things,
not least (if, finally, *that's* a word here)
all the unbroken attention …

Fuelled, the Indian Pacific thrums.
I pick myself up toweringly.
The true star laughs half to death.

Sand slogs on by political sidings, Watson scab-red as skins of servicemen,
Maralinga Tjarutja exposed, denied by Old Blighty's Black Mist. 'Keep Out':
Maralinga, place of thunder, radioactive for the Melbourne Olympics.

Six golds to the Mother Country, a deal for seven bombs; armchair
expertise wears thin where the going rate's fifty years of lies. Opposite
hop auburn flurries so 'at it' we only aim more weapons at ourselves.

Post-lunch announcements herald convoys, a tin of milo tossed
to Ziggy the Hermit's corrugated keep. Flagging, I scan the scarlet dunes
once terraformed to fit the line (word from the Western Front by camel,

a 'triumph of civilisation' declared as corpses filled the digs of France).
Uneven gauges forced interruptions. In '35, a young Doug Nicholls,
Big V wingman, saw his people run to beg. On him, it made its mark ...

Sunset picks the brains of scrub, receding thoughts of Daisy Bates,
'the black man's friend', Irish anthropologist, making it up as she
went along. She loved lost words ('mis-ce-ge-na-tion'), stuck it out where I

sail through. But why predict the end of anyone from a place that holds
your gaze around the outer, reigns supreme in a star-kissed harshness,
claims not merely by comparison—a faceless primacy not always into you?

Fixed stars crowning open dark:
Port Augusta is a revelation.
Infrastructure's grimy haloes

crowd around an ocean mirror,
offering themselves glass grapes.
How we fete hyperfunctional vanity,

floodlights, even the cold!
        Things falling in on themselves
dressed as people huddle, cough,

Steve their zombie raconteur.
A disembodied hoot: *Seen the toilets?*
Shades in a minor stampede.

Two murals occupy the breezeway:
land, sky spirits; Afghan cameleers.
        Sit, we're told. *We'll be here*

for a while. Vertical, then,
by the phlegm of the near, I wake
to the blue rasp of whale country.

No dreams tonight, just Adelaide: its hills a smudge of nightclub glitter,
old rooves clench their tin.   Something unglued survives by velocity.
How to pass? (Yours, a Lawrence of Erasure, jacket on head against

breath-frosted glass). Grey sisters prop up their ancient father, one cradles
his temple and texts.   Doors part to three degrees in the eyes, mercy
familial under the terminal which brekky line ladies dole out and invite.

Bundled up in a train platform,
gobsmacked at the world:
your mother gave you

eyes of the dawn, bubbles
to postulate warmth for your head;
abracadabras outconjuring air,

casting and snatching threads
far from my grasp, but you know
where they are, it's no secret.

    OO

warmth—you're it. In secret, bub,
you train the dawn-bundled air threads
up from a platform of Mother

to where they postulate no
snatching head. Your abracadabras
forgave my far world,

but grasp, gobsmacked,
at the casting eyes, bells
you know and are outconjuring.

Third day, northbound from the City of Churches. Gullied golden beads
on clay. We're rag-tag, the few left blearily empty. The new commandant
makes his presence felt: *Your full attention is a privilege, not a right.*

I run a tight ship, no drugs or grog. With me you'll get off quick smart.
He won't count two nights' prior uprightness: *Feet off the seats,
you can't sleep like that.* I think my eyes are now some kind of gas.

A Martian ochre swallows all. Flinders Ranges are migratory whales
caught in a synchronised dive! From their titanic wind-pocked humps,
emus glare at a screeching thing, as they did for Sturt and his whaleboat

to scurvy, fame, a sealed highway—anything but an inland sea.
Death condemned him, nearly knighted, to drink himself to myth
in Port Adelaide (there's the plan and there's what happens to the plan).

The track forgets, shoves strangers together, the worst so far
in close, fierce arbitration. Darwin fishos trap Dutch Florian:
What's a test-tube baby's worst nightmare? A dingo with a straw.

I drown it half out with old lasered revelries (Digweed, Underworld),
chittering tempos in thumping thrall; loops and drops crossfaded,
layered, easing as our thread resumes, but doubtful now the people ...

Winking scrub slows to mullock heaps, the man-made mesas of Broken Hill;
its iron cathedral with a total view for those who never came home.
Sky in the trees sees everything cease. Sky whizzing with the opposite of stones.

We totter from our snorting hellride.
Pretty quiet on a school day,
skate park, Christian bookshop at the strip.

My lone souvenir is *Bad Girls of the Bible
and What We Can Learn from Them*
in staunch softcover.

Under my lids, a burning rain
veils spaces between thoughts and God's.
Nothing more floods.

How did I make my last time on again?
Skewed outlines clack to sheep and roos
quenched intermingling around the one flaming dam.

Dark passage doesn't have to mean a thing. It has taken itself well from you.
Left before. Are you its sullen bouncing baby, rockabyed, and yet a wraith?
The wraith has almost deathless wisdom, its simple cost a lightening

of self, which you maintain (and maintain!) has more grounding.
The juddering of flattened stars feels loosely on your side. They're cold
to your nose, the living one, pressed up to clown your way out. No dice.

Your dual-paned, deadpan wraith keeps thin. Brow of your brow,
mask of your mask. A floating stencil in the silver gallery's facing walls
of shades rugged up and butterfly-lidded, jolting worlds out of sight.

     The wraith keeps up. It can and will. It crinkles, fades for a braggart
crossing in place of a mortal grin. Place doesn't have to mean a thing.
And now you've lied to your final friend, except, of course, the stinging

dark, but who can meet on such poor terms, lashed to a cloud called
New South Wales, bursting east on driest spells, serried bulbs without
foundation?   Except, except. The gnash of the train. Heels, hips

and blood. *Except, except …* You fought and flew in rolling motion,
broke live dreams for a second's composition. You fade to an age where
the wraith is still watching. You sing to your only one: *Back in an instant.*

I prise my jowl from the frozen aisle where I slept like a drooling dog
(and well), slink to my seat under cover of dark.   Floating tones
as a few kick on, slugs of hip flasks in the vampiric pre-dawn descent

from the Blue Mountains cut. Wine-dark clouds sop the mouths
of cauldrons. *Minus six out.* None the stomach to contend.
      Pathetic wafts from chimneys snake a plunging bark necropolis;

slate-grey trunks alit, washed fresh. Pupil-high, through my tightening
window, silver supplications stream gum, snail beaded scripts.
      I shut my eyes to last night's streetlamps, truck-stops choked

by cosmic foliage, grids of moth-manic towns. Soon, I'll be waiting
at the doorframe's glow to step from this fugitive spook story,
rearranged despite my flesh.   We jag and slide and churn

for the newborn sun, a near-blind finicky creature licking off shadows
of afterbirth, density smoothed away to the edge of its being, slathered
with dripping warmth.   Structures now. Night collects its effects.

      The breakfast crowd looks shot, subdued, like death warmed up
(some twit has to rib), wiping their isometric mouths at early hours
with shops, graffiti, bridges, rubbish, eggs on toast. Escape cannot be

a constant costume, persevere all we may (on the way).   The West
retracts, retracts to Gallipoli Mosque's minarets, burnished high-rises
of the clipped Inner West, their bonsai awakenings at first senescence.

Marty at Last

The doors hiss apart and there's Marty,
a mate I've never known *not* to be there.
We met before I held memory
as a toy to tamper with (and how),
at playgroup in the lore of two families
and, since, of each other's reality.
I shone at inviting myself around,
now to this hitherto mythical city
I breezed through once as a child.

We're equally crumpled, black-haired
and brown, laughing through tubes
of echo and shadow, phalanxes
of public despair. In the company car
(coffee by the Suhartos), Marty
warns me *It's crazier here:*
five-way intersections, summer storms;
get stuck in a tunnel and you're
a lamb to the slaughter.

His windscreen beeps in shrill assent
and we're lifted in bumping lanes
of sheet music, connective crescendos
of girders, beams. *It's weird*
how fast you learn to ignore it ...
Marty sardonically loves his boss,
who clocks off after the Monday
rev-up, an old rep's odes
to the Paul Hogan days in tobacco,
Kings Cross on the company card.

I'll stick to trains in a sea of ink,
hit independent bookshops for shifts,

my casual life on A4. I wrangle
a word from Marty's order pad.
*Ar-TAR-Mon. And that's just
the start of it...!* He swings us
down a purple portal, crashing off
bumps they call Silent Policemen.

Eastern States

Sydney Central Again

The citadel is bristling
    curlicues of vanished trains
standard issue altruism
clanking altered bolt and thread
    droning on
we can't leave alone
        necked, overblown
    warding off black holes
a cube root of the Hadron Collider
I'll never make it outside
    white-tiled exposure
By the time I've taken
        the streets veer off
    pin-cushion ears
rips and pops of
streaming schoolgirls
    museums of wind
who vaunt and decry their own
    with every look
foaming at the mouth it seems a
    cracking 7-11 fluorescence

transplant-fortified capitulations
    deviate through lunglike mazes
shouldering the wave machine
    rescheduled closer
the Benevolent Asylum
        sips of breaking point
forgive each case of the bottomless pits
    with pinging toys
        or dust
    worn to the central
transients bunched sleeping rough
    second thoughts twice
        into lateral vertigo
    suspect schizotourism
Hyde Park bats jostling, heckling
    the Pool of Remembrance
laser-sharp throngs
        roaring shadows
you have to buy this
    coke to live with any taste
your scratched face stealing from a fridge

Department of Someones

I   Mutual Obligation

A different window, one taped with a sign. Someone wanted. Apply within. We pick up the action late in the final term.

How would you describe your experience?
Everyone I've met is from somewhere else, running on empty for a moment alone.

Riiight. [Sideways glance.] How again are you someone?
Someone told me.

So you've put down. But how do you know *they* were someone?
They were most qualified in someoneness.

Sounds suspiciously null.
I thought it was real.

No! Nothing ever is with you!
Well, how do you know that you're someone?

Clearly, I'm a figment of an imagination you don't yet possess, but to think like that you'd have to, on the outside, first be nothing.
But it said apply within ...

Fantastic.

[Nothing moves.]

II   Turning It On/Off Again

Another day where you trick the computer to think like you / if you were a more pliant plant / but you're not / so you drag yourself to subsistence / thinking the whole thing's absurd and out of the blue you can't stop braying with laughter / doubling over in a public thoroughfare / rolling and patting out fire from the sky / or life behind light / to be filmed / pointed at / You recover in time for the relevant authorities not to have to record anything / lope round the corner / smash a six-dollar soup / Holes in your free bread / all free bread / Dirt in your phlegm and risen blood / a surface scrape down your mouse-hand / You once read the vision went viral in China / but it never quite dropped / popped / lit up your socials and you're laughing less now anyway

III   Read All the Mags Twice

Well it's got to be said if it's worth doing once, it's worth doing
well, but there are only so many times you can go to the
well if you look at the great acting performances,
well there's always Brando, who told Johnny Depp: Tears
well, we fill. What's the point of
well-rounded performances, when you know as
well as I do what the audience hates and when you're
well-off you become them. Part of you must forever starve in the stair-
well of your first audition, a
well-cut breakdown from the method school. Helps if you're not
well to start with, dysfunctional. Like bloody here. Read all the mags twice.
Well, for best actress, why not Jodie Foster's
well-documented clash with Robert Downey Jr who was starring as
well in *Home for the Holidays* and pretty, you know,
well-gone on the drugs, zooming a little space shuttle in his trailer when
Well, what the hell, broke in Jodie, *might as*
well spill—what is the reason for this major behaviour?
(Well, she directed, but I liked her in *Nell*). *I'll get Sean Penn to sort you*
well out mate, good luck with the shuttle program ...
Well, Penn cracks it, leather jacket: *Time to pay the piper!* Downey's
well now, 'on a journey', franchise favourite.
Well, who'd be an actor, these days anyway. It's all
well and good partying with
well-wishers, producers, heiresses ... but I'd take this life, no bull!
Well, you're not me. You'd hit the
well like your arse was on fire, mate. I know you too
well, that's my never-ending punishment.

IV   JobSeeker: A Counter-Demand Letter

These are the people
prosperity scatters
to scrape about
fistless in the dust
(as I was).

Not a mote
may be misappropriated,
disassociated,
underquoted
on the cashless life.

Now we want
their fists, of course.
The algorithm
hates them.
Ruin tastes thinner

than sweetened death
we shelve ourselves,
devise to hide it,
while the rest
insist they feed

or last or breed
by recollection
of unbroken nights
of feasts. Of a time
they once showed

plenty and that plenty
could afford them,
need them not

like a hole
in the head,

but I guess like
neighbours used to.
Some still might
in the real world
(Yours etc).

V   Scant

She walks barefoot in the cut and rush,
she's learned to walk, remind
through people, barefoot,
as they walk through people,
bared and fooled behind.

In each case, feet set the story:
riven skin on luckless bone,
she feels each sole in the tug
of another, a dance to the sound
that calls the steps home.

Pivots scum. Staccato, stiletto,
the well-heeled lunch crowd
snakes a cracked whip;
upper crusts scolding, flashing about
her hearing back, tough underneath.

Today is not to be pocket dialled
or tired, touching base in the lifts.
She prays and she presses,
divines the right path.
Serious. Consumed. Everlasting.

South a Little

Oscillating tiger stripes of ochre
      line the way
as we impatient urban damned
      descend around, around
to the river coursing cold
      through fractured marri's
loosened, spiralling boats.

We arrive submerged in our dusts
      to smuggled thunder,
seal-black rock of a water chamber
      with its mists
playing up like a sozzled comic:
      rainbows worming
russet froth beneath the freak
      intensive flow
oceanward from a gutted scarp.

Here in this euphoric skull
      of an old system
we've never been
      louder, less
ourselves, or machines.

Blanket

Few will admit to harbouring an umbrella
and if they do, someone they don't talk that much to
or a dead neighbour who blotted their copybook
donkey's years back left it parched on the hook.

Now meteorologists are Satan's butlers in bow ties,
mumbling to parrots who know how to fall,
but not as light from rebellion in heaven
remembered today by the ritual mislaying,

denial of our fellow souls' shields, condemned
to inner racks and nooks. (It never rains in Sydney,
or there'd have to be awnings, contingencies,
some kind of indoor culture). Repent, my cough,

rain entire in itself is parent over our babbling city.
We reach too slow in appointed bone corridors,
ancient crevasses that swoon if provoked
by witless mentions of the Great Enclosing.

It's dark we're so down on the Destroyer
of Parties patting us clean with fragrant base soils
if, by our drives, we confess our thrills ...
Hush, new molecules are sprinkling.

You Yangs and Diving Boards

Waves, gravitational
mind-mussings teem,
plunge for the jewel
in the clouds and hit clean.

Car-roar obvious,
where can it bring?
You Yangs are slumbering,
no slumbering thing.

Refineries, youths
to the ultramarine,
excite to become what they
thought they could beam—

low-lidded cirrus,
a hole in a dream
sucked from the slumberers'
chimney-staked sheen.

At Nan Tien Temple, Wollongong

Late fire in my tea
turns four eagles, me.

Look, no hands, just you
and you looking down

no sea, no shadow briefly
well enough alone.

A wrinkle of steam fears
the courtyard unwritten,

bleeds a rolling note
of this impermanence

up from my interlaced grip—
then only now being born.

Creature Quatrains

Thy
Three magpies clip, triangulate cirrus over a paddock
of monochrome cows. A thylacine slinks, nonchalant,
through the fenceline. *You've got to be kidding,*
my dream-ire scoffs. *No*, says the thylacine. *No I'm not.*

Dragonfly
Asterisk to an Autumn promise,
metallic green with a rubied shadow,
I'm hovering wild, gyrating vibrato
hooked and flung by a last claw of wind.

Glebe Island Ibis
How nights have flown, and commuted forgiveness
winds to a slow somnambulant strictness
snaking its way in a tussle of song to a keeper of eels
beyond the beyond ... dioxins, radium.

Roo
A 'divine mistake' your first biblical poet proclaimed as 'boomers',
'flyers', 'joeys' were unceremoniously tagged and founded.
Books omit how we shot from your pages, sensing our beat renewed us.
Now we're farmed for our excellent meat, but you're off the unbounded.

Hyde Park Fruit Bat
Geckoesque suncrawlers grip to glass
in haunting procession with tails in a case,
pinned ears and all that upscale hoo-ha. Coats ludicrous
when sweat made you kings. Scowling, invertible kings.

Hospital Pigeon
To not sit among other people's aloneness
once is the polished hope
clouded with language
they swing silver trolleys on, exiting density.

Spider's Shell
Huntsman, your shining prophetess
I am, ensnared for one last movement
of a hypothesis called death.
There, you can't disprove it.

Lyrebird
So a quilled mimic's more wayer than farer;
I can sing planes with a scrape of the foot,
rewrite syrinx-strains no starling could.
Back to the wings, ye minor player.

Skeeter
I fade into corners, you snap on a light
sans fascicle and culex, true,
but game enough for my accusations—
youuuuuu times ten to the power. Flat.

Snail
If the soul is female,
I'm cross-dressing just being here.
Parthenogenesis is next to godliness.
The oracle was the volcano.

Rooster
I don't know when it was
I was apprenticed to oblivion.
Little matter ... raucous,
open-ended, filling in.

Stromatolites
Even three billion rounds of the sun
remind us not enough,
in truth, of how our
niche reigns—stony, ceremonially.

Worker Ants
Onwards unsweetened by poison and powder,
old wives' concoctions our lover eludes;
missing a segment we carry each other
like sugar for valour, for instinct, for food.

City Ringtail
We're mercifully blind in a stargazing thrill
with damp litter licking its leaves up at us.
Each nears to need, needs to near, *so*.
Good and evil grow quiet here.

Chimp
I accept, as babe and elder
of delight's dry clan. You, sir,
have been touched by genius.
Let me shake your hand.

Kookaburra
Beneath bellbirds' circumcommunicado,
stink bugs mate, reversed, on a leaf. Heh!
Families of finches spiral the backwater.
Hollowed trees conduct the swift river.

Pacific Long-Haul Raptures

Agate and filmy stellate crusts like the first amphibian
(yours too), speculating itself clear of nightfall's
pounding ossuary ... I was or wasn't around, Half-Planet,
depths and folds we mustn't know; if the tall are prone
disentangle them completely from each trident-shaped
break from homing. Above the New Hebrides Trench,
wisps less laughable than firmament close out
roughcut paper in photonegative, furrowed grain
through the gloom. Before a Hawaii I never see,
netting or losing a day is direction, instrumental in a desert
of cloud (and deserts of continents are each a Pacific).
Your calendared hermaphrodite rides sidesaddle
crying wingtip light at the wonkiest point
of our tumbling cage: one bar loose to squint again, off,
at the cold diversion of a monocled Greenwich
who calls himself prime down your full turning back.

Encased museum whispers of the sky world flit the masks
of particoloured non-complaint binding sunken sorrow.
Surfacing all golden-eyed, they shield themselves
with infant hands, plug to something in their laps
or spurn announcements, then in French,
to sever open glory lest their waxen slack-jawed
memberships to numinous imposture fail. Sleepers
paw at rays the very disc-clouds bear in numbers.
Above (you choose) the Solomons, lilac streaks
hone cometlike to pinking cuttlefish quills.
You, Half-Planet, hide upon, below, as a wreathed
blue range and a wing. Canadian birds fly arrowhead V's,
Australians in loose barometric sheathes, and so they hang
cross-hatched in economy, ruffling wavy suns
which burst clipped dreams then return to you proudly.

Translated Cranes

Changchung's the long Spring we lost in a day.
How do the birds go without? And where are they?
Pyongyang a crow's Vladivostok away.
Blossoms wince from thin ice, breaking news.

How do the birds go without? And where are they?
Cranes are those consummating construction.
Blossoms wince from thin ice, breaking news
pink down the spine of Jilin University.

Cranes are those consummating construction
of language. Just as my luggage is slipping
pink down the spine of Jilin University,
concrete launches a mummified sun.

Language, just as my luggage, is slipping,
live, relayed through black padded headphones.
Concrete launches a mummified sun.
Friends, we sacrificed our environment ...

Live, relayed through black padded headphones,
mistranslations randomise suitably:
Friends, we sacrificed our environment;
eat and drink to your heart's continent.

Mistranslations randomise suitably,
flower together in our severe future,
eat and drink to our heart's continent.
Caked minibus panes at particulate dusk

flower together in our severe future.
State TV blasts airspace lies of US puppet Japan.

Caked minibus panes at particulate dusk
ghost plumed ravines, shrines to live escalation.

State TV blasts airspace lies of US puppet Japan;
Pyongyang, a crow's Vladivostok away,
ghosts plumed ravines, shrines to live escalation.
Changchung's the long Spring we lost in a day.

The Professor and The Unnamed Stalk the Post-Apocalyptic Wilderness

So much is silent beyond sand and men
with pronouncements, low strains whipping
at our boots. Furs, exposed skin slipping
from remnants quietly when
fierceness can't stand the pathogen
of recollection's ravenous gripping.
Now we hunt lizards, re-arming, re-equipping,
in this arrestedness once called unbroken.
We surface no more to the grey names of lovers,
but flit, intercept—miniature as a shadow—
death through heretical ruins of the plateau
lacing to cradle our breath again,
as moss seeps lush from a crevice, recovers
a beauty which misses us as we did oxygen.

Earthly Delights

I   Perennial

To not give yourself to the red and grey heart
of another (or your own) is a terrible risk.

Chance, vulnerability stalk the unexposed.
Predictable safety, being born and not

plunging once, stonelike, from a shivering nest
through the dread of your gut is risk past redress.

Knowing to whom you give by what
they do not show the stars or sands,

but retrieve by dreamtide of morning
—gold wine tilting through a chalice of gravity—

that runs the risk of a planetary happiness
which is intoxicating, quickening drowsiness.

II   Cetacean Bosch

No bones in the ground to be local enough,
but I heard *Count the spouts* from a bearded watcher
of heaving coves, gun range to Lady Bay.
He wouldn't expand, having spoken.

From his denuded ridge of sun, I made out
sixty-six Southern Rights (figments?), thronging
inversions as Hirry B saw: expressionless juveniles
corkscrewing orange into displacements of glitter

and gulls; larger, brine-sleeved flippers,
all detail, whomping down on their knobbly heads.
The watcher, lifted and framed by his landing,
feels equal parts pain and flawed design

for lustrous birds of fable and oil, their afterbirth
or nutrient slick, for our sake lost to lamps and corsets.
Calves, through the garbled vastness now,
clad themselves in barnacled sun, his tiny sable grin.

Should we rush their laden singing,
Blues rebuff our landed sight as vessels track
mammalian raptures down to a pressurised
feasting blank that's nothing to meditate to.

III   East
i.m. Lucas North

From thin smacking rockpools
I stare out the Heads
and the Harbour skin is growing in tune.
Spray takes a temporary
break from fatalism, scales pink stone
parapets round The Gap. A first
wriggle of snorkelers, cormorants,
shades … What is the brain
a metaphor for? Sea can't tell
if it's poem or poet; face
scoops along in burnished drag.
A dazzling darkness
roams each side of dawn.

'Reality is a hologram you can
put your arm through'
(memory's catch of your lines, Lucas,
your voice, each erasing
wash of you). *It's hell to be a writer
in Perth*, I'd gloomed
once, under the Reid Library.
*It's hell to be a writer
anywhere,* you shot back; committed,
we both fell about
and you gave me a tape of German
industrial that out-
clanged my wicked Pulsar.

Then your name, and it couldn't
be real—*Cricketer's
Brother Killed on Perth Freeway.*
I pick at rock with

a stammering breath. Currawongs
dart yellow-eyed
from antennae. You ran out of fuel
in that desolate canyon
('Writers and their cars,' we'd laughed).
You were the first
on my small way to hand me writing
that was never a choice.

I always saw how we'd meet again
wrong, in shards
of an ivied azure courtyard,
or verandah where
you lent your time. We'd mock our
weird congratulations,
reinforce each other—*Sure!*—plumb
again the one conversation
worth humouring, ashen, inward,
with a sideways grin,
with dazzling darkness roamed
each side of dawn.

Reporting the World: John Pilger Exhibition

Blood or ash or slasher film,
it matters not when you ask
the rubble. When you ask the birds.

The disappeared are everywhere.
Their freezeframed siege (mock
absolution) out of it, subject

to execution, but they are more
lucid than you. They know the sums
can be done now without them.

Tuol Sleng, 1979: *Twenty thousand …*
eight survivors … four kids and
a one-month-old baby. Forensic

sunlight sifts through splattered
papershrouds of floor. Beneath
the insect bedframe, chains

and ties, an upturned coffee cup
revolves in a resinous swamp:
routine where the screams

punched through this earth's
collected tufts of hair to stars
still swallowing unfocused.

At the Non-Existent Statue of a Speared Arthur Phillip

I

The first drunks of Summer
are windily weaving,
and windily leaving
their minds from a can.

An empty, kicked somewhere,
skids phonically, pleading.
Public profanity
is the new placelessness:

Weak prick!
Go hard or go home.
(But the dead!).

The local prime member shrinks,
does himself in, wades on,
shark-toothed at the scent
of blent victimhood.

Scull, get stuck in
blue fire, white wharf
as another ramp crashes
and tongues of the earth

loosen to swim
in their
version of it.

II

It never costs nothin' to go to the beach,
gleams a freed, ecstatic man
to his family.

Steyne means stone. Heads over water
in hours only stone hears,
featureless, dim.

Pines relieved of their birdsong,
crawling. On, or over
the line,

promised touch— pigment where
there's a skin
again.

III

Again, Phillip advanced,
playing father,
chiding and soothing
his pre-arranged
wounding.

His sentencing judge,
the esteemed Willemaring,
yells stay in the dock,
take up spear
or club;

Bennelong, your honourable
Counsel Assisting,

is just as impossible,
healed smooth
to prove it.

No contest?
No more will
you not
get the
point.

IV

Point, pistol, pox, plinth,
picnic, pub, parade.
'Seven miles from Sydney
and a thousand miles from care'.
The gilled Pacific nips

plaques for Olympians,
mixed bathing pervs
and a frilled Georgian
Bennelong, underfoot,
outside McDonald's.

Bricked-down languages,
local and Latin, share
*whale (gawura, megaptera
novaeangliae)* as they
could share the sea.

A whale feast here, meat
—'Mate' as recorded—
canoed to the po-faced father

of *galgalla* and much let
between *supply* and *deploy.*

Incisions, middens,
bloodlines persist.
Tides mark the deep
passing through
of continuance.

V

Continuance now has a countenance, contrivance:
Bath boy of German Jakob, Lizzy Breach,
the little breacher bronzed on his block
of this block-headed Ice-Aged sea dragon of land.

Rendered due east, Willemaring's tip west
juts like a beak from the governor's spine;
harbour sparks hook up his wreck of a shoulder,
ride its reverberant shaft to the pines.

Long bicorn hat unbelievably fastened,
head thrown back, but his face—we can know
the face—imminent, bulging, eyes flung agog
in a heaven of surprise. Thin rhomboid lips

frame a right missing tooth (Art's fluke),
flashing golden abandon at those who'll recover
from physical laws, inscrutable yet as the surf
or the Feds fanging arcs in their black ops boats—

not the friends of late lanced circulations
changing states of the glazed drawn to linger.
Winter. Masts lash for Art each electric night;
rocked just like his condescending sight.

Ultraviolet Dusk Before a Storm

Radiance vies to stream from itself:
an incandescent impressionist house
above the constricting deep
of the valley. Fluoro pink,
its bark belies no actual
Child-of-the-Good-type sun.

A birdless hush in nostrils, drums,
dilates like the mauve dry earth;
forest floors upswept electric
but for a sudden candied orange
half-light of retreating time,
blasting fleshy paranormal
gutter leaves aglow and on.

The ultraviolet void is perfect,
not that the other world wasn't,
but it wouldn't wait for us.
The ultraviolet void is waiting only:
bones eventuate through dark
suspensions of the clearing south
to reaches, skins, our found indigoed eyes.

Thirteen Ways of Sighing in an Ecocide

After Wallace Stevens

Waves sigh and crumble
at Newport Beach. Phantasms of mist
twist off like smoke won't.

On a soft-sand jog
I bury four cormorants, lift them
on driftwood where grains spin and sigh.

Worsening news and a worsening sky.
I can't tell if it sighs.
The wind dies, is death.

Twilight from three
is one kind of future (and sigh).
Sunnies on, both again.

North Sydney's Cloud City
from *The Empire Strikes Back*;
I feel its captive carbon sighs
climb my eery skin.

Tomato vines sag and sigh,
won't fruit, choke
like outdoor children.

We sigh and accept
the sun is the moon
in this
taming of us—
mask reversed, a frantic air.

The PM's office denies
he's in Hawaii, sighs
It's not a story. Nice try.

My New Year's dream
beside a blood-red feed:
a sphere crowned by haze
in the sigh of space
relies on us more than we do.

Remind me now
how love
confounds the powerful.
Sighs carry accents,
a stroke of your hair.

A billion lives?
No sigh on earth
exists for this.
For insects, countless.
Save one without end.

A silver morning's soundless sigh.
Could azure breach
October's strikes, shadow and light
sit apart at funerals?

A sigh of rain no minor godsend,
but some old frogs sing.
When this Summer's buried,
I must warn the cormorants
under the sand or clear sky
it rests with them.

Contagion

Strange
         pavement, unchanged—

my mask,
         my misanthropy

shrivel
         something cruel

Cottesloe Nights

Rematerialised

Sweet shape on riderless waves
tonight, barrelling gasps of space

with a little more body. Christmas,
Antarctica, Aceh, Sri Lanka,

the great white shark highway
to Africa, quite a left-hander ...

Pumping, my home in its Western form.
Rank desiccations at the plane door.

Relative

Laugh. Be done. Plod milky cool
of distance ripped enough to kiss off,
sunspot galaxies frothing language,
streets ossified by the slightest hex.

Night knows we lose ourselves
to the nanosecond; space hangs
its paintings for days we will look
with space. Cry, the next feared seed's

upswelling to play absolutes
(everyone gets fried) in cracking bones,
beery globes, rows of stones down
the great south land of the Mooro clan

of the Whadjuk Noongar. Vlamingh
slipped from his croaking monsters
near where my shoeless forebears strolled,
rumours of Japanese caches patrolled

to truceless hours by the SAS, dugites,
breaks the dead to the world flinch under,
genuflections of Seconds, The Cove,
nude beach paling to an ambient Floreat.

Holographic

Had to return before I felt it again
when out late—there's nobody coming.
No drunks, no cops, no tattooed swells,
it's not relative, just abandoned stellate salve
for glass from sand, sand from shell,
shell from animal. For all the little jellied
microbes dosed in their triple-glazed homes.
For gulls jagging mist and lip so low
spume pitches from their wings.

In Freo Maritime Museum floats Megamouth,
resplendent green in a chamber of ooze:
the five-metre freak shark gaping soft terror
at each treasured body's glued non-response.
The concourse palls. At crack of dawn,
do cleaners kneel, beseech Megamouth?
Its legend spat from the maw of the deep
like Cottesloe nights, returned lifeproof.
This nineteen seventy-six conception
unknown longer than the coelacanth.

Gull

As a flock's one wide formation,
motion wiles itself from the one.
For one more turn of the wind and sun,

we would pass your face through
the peering froth, a falling dream
a flying dream. Shake!

If you catch the ghosts of fish
to pocket them in a higher stream,
be careful what you wish.

We've Gone and

When the government calls time at 10pm
so the rough-as-guts can hold it down
Monday, I find my way to a third state.

The bell-shaped Pylon, shark net relic,
sports floodlit gauze with a Wadjemup brooch,
skips moon rocks where an old mouth fell:

the Pre-Swan, bioluminescent. Raked
with light from the tourist gulag, Southern
Cross awkward is the new 2am: its five eyes

(guns, grain, gold, iron, tellie) burn aggro,
more substance-abused than I left them
upside-down by the reap of Peter's Pool.

Crowns amass in the festive sea lane. Baubles
of dew bow spinifex shoots like the backs
of far men noosed, chained and starving.

Stripped Back

All day the sky tangled red wind and blue,
birds pulled their proverbs out of the sky.
The tension turns murderous: choppers
flog sideways, coral trees petition dust.
Streets away, a car alarm screams
Hide me, hide me, hide me. Litter skips
perfumed magenta. Nape fur cricks.
Is the power out? Rolling bellyaches
gain imploringly from a skin too sour to see,
pricked stratospheric mood-flesh creeping,
tuning to our own. It agonises down
upon us: panes convulse, we flare, count up;
backs of hot eyes ionise to the front.
Howls as the re-earthed shrouds.

Seconds

Winter's gift is a skyward fin unable to halt
its plea; a bus-sized belly, pale as karri,
gently puppeteered by the chop. Its
upturned stave, alien to wind but
for the full breach of youth,
slides synoptic. Bowls of
lost flesh and a day-old
stench made noonday
conditional, so the
town came.

Slain
crescent tail,
parkaed Easter
Island statues on
gobsmacked cliffs
in the sour amber spray
are just as they are, no more
frightening. Winter's gift still slaps
at its reef bed, trying to roll out of a dream.

Tracking

Don't like it, leave!
        Pedestrian spray
at a faint zebra crossing
        has a bit each way.

Outlying waters
        strike and whip,
paralyse the distant ships,
        setting them

from where they queued
        to suckle the horizon.
Megamouth floats
        over years and cars,

trails spectral greens
        less ghostly
than I'd find myself,
        eighteen and over-

subscribed in
        intelligent life,
hugging a coat down
        a dead Marine Parade.

The freak shark slows,
        agape, to a hover,
swivels fins to dive,
        kiss the earth ...

A single fish skin
        nudges roadside,

fattens, spinning to tide.
       More tooth-picked

bones wriggle down.
       Then crest by chin,
the sea's taken begin:
       sloshing hessian,

grins and caps;
       trudging, slapping
on wet backs, they
       return as in a dream,

which, not too cruel,
       both loved and left them
clear, never knowing
       when they started.

Footage

Then the still. Macerated yellow weeds
surf night-cart lanes for old failings of breeze
from sparking roads, off-white homes, cyclone wire
explaining cruel-to-be-kind housing prices
to chip-wrap caught in the shallows of space
over spat change. (I have changed, remained the same).

Before the Tuscan mansions came,
limestone rocks in every street were perfect
for drawing, fighting or writing with.
Cott Civic Centre's whooshing pine castle,
where I learnt to hide, now fields motion sensors,
cameras. (And seek. Stars drink back the partition).

Blue weatherboard husks and their
armoured replacements blanch like mining
trucks stoned, with retic. North, where
my high school stood before the sandfire
noon eclipse closed in, they taught small 'i's,
the impossible numbers. (And how we could just say no).

They never taught bullant or birdshadow,
'dusky types' (so called) expelled to Bassendean,
if you have to know. Small 'i's cancelling
was a last lesson. That calculus now has eaten
my school. A drive-in chained out-of-bounds served
as classic. (Derros wagging vegie maths ashed there).

Don't switch off yet. Impossible numbers still
have their tricks, an unreal engineering.
How the hell else could they halfway exist?
How did I know this and not, at sixteen,

who Swanway Crescent's memorial crosses
now project? (Where a chain fence snaked before).

Streetlight hits them like a kind of pain.
They radiate back dignity from cold metal.
Here are some of the sharp-browed people,
their fair and terrible words. I should have played
with their grandkids, taken in more than
a gnawing absence, death. (It's now and it's never too late).

Dumped

I

Each dumped figure makes a unique shape,
slung through zero-G foam and shadow,

arse over tit in counter-revolution,
the prospect of oxygen taken as a comment.

Wiped out / hammered / pummelled / nailed /
cactus / ragdolled / pounded / eaten / owned ...

Spray-crested mountains bulge to the bay,
tessellate down to a single sentience.

From first thing, say. Older moons, iron suns
in the main to us. Burst to suck a skyful—just.

II

Animal, mineral silence
bordered unsuccessfully as waves.
Gated lashes, nostrils, tongues:
no wonder first impressions bathe,
grizzling to a cratered pool
before their lengths might care to vary.
Knowing now they're asking for it.
Knowing now it's temporary.

Skip a smooth stone clear enough,
it coils into a tail. Lines which
never fail steal home, tentacular,
lapping the murk by a touch.
Crystalline days no memory equals,
languorous distances stored
in the skin ... it's kind no one knows
all of a life, so each outstrips
this grey-nursed, spilling body.

Where Our

Bipeds living separate lives emote securely to a circle of screens.
Keypads flash down Loma Street walls in red and green
ersatz shipping lanes. Occupy space. Hypnotise. Lay waste,

like the first sold a shooter's paradise—kangaroos, bronzewings
splashing from jarrah and wattle of quarried North Cottesloe,
that feral, goannaed 'Siberia'. Then teamsters, gamblers, camel races,

picnicked attempts at a rabid Brighton (white baby contests
for unsecured plots); Noongar, West Indian, Chinese hawkers
with spices, sponges, contraptions, fisherfolk trading shock

at that attack, the look of the kid hauled grey from a dancing
bosom meant to cure everything. Jetty bands, parlour cars,
a twelve-foot tiger strung pointedly—attractions worth queuing for.

'Costume, Men and Women: Dress of dark material, serge, flannel
or flannelette extending from the shoulder to the knee. Those in
swimsuits should not loiter.' This was before the advent of the groyne.

Sun Sets in a

Cott burns, radiates, has a pen for its name
or escape artist's cradle (in the sun's breath,
mein Gott). In blood-red sea, a haloed beginning
greets its wandering rhyme in the flames
while deathsalt, lifesalt squirm hand in hand
from lorikeet cries to replies of clean release.

A shark cull carries the day. Plug, release
offence from above, armed love tough to name.
Just grant us this day to be again swum, hand
round the ultra-high spectrum and breathe
grainily like a prostrate lizard, *hah*. Spray flames
wild where teen bombers explode, beginning

again up The Pylon's spike. In the beginning
were tin men, horsies, scrapes. No release
comes close to the first haring down in flames,
caught in a soft teal kerchief by (stage name)
Indian O. Panthalassa, (occupation) breath-
catching fire eater, mesmerist, marvel. *A hand*

for my assistants ... You truly have to hand
it to them once you're under: flesh beginning
to cup vital currents, prisms that breathe
the way of corals harvest moons release.
*Without them I saw myself in half, to name
but a few inconsistencies.* Brine heals, inflames

surface wounds scab-pink like the sun. Flames
of street barbies whoosh brightly out of hand.
A fin on one, unfoiled from the beginning,
sizzles, curls prehensile. Does it bid no name

of its own, no crisp reaction past that release
dried children down, holding its breath?

Forget. From the train, tangerine we breathe
in bobbing lines up Forrest Street, which flames
to the last crow's nest. Why dash home, release
choked extremities? Cott, don't you hand
us back. I see light's amoebalike core beginning
to bind, multiply with a craft none can name ...

My shortness of breath is the length of your name
in plumed release, giving out like a hand
and mind in flames, taken down—my beginning.

Notes

Indian Pacific
Historical passengers include engineer C.Y. O'Connor (1843–1902), gold prospector Paddy Hannan (1840–1925), explorers Edward John Eyre (1815–1901) and Minang Noongar man Wylie (precise years unknown), Yorta Yorta state footballer, pastor, activist and South Australian Governor Sir Douglas Nicholls (1906–1988), welfare worker and anthropologist Daisy Bates (1863–1951), explorer Charles Sturt (1795–1869). You Am I is an Australian rock band fronted by Tim Rogers. Freud made his remarks in his 1928 essay 'Dostoevsky and Parricide'. TRG is the acronym for the Tactical Response Group police unit. A TPI ex-serviceperson is one classified as Totally and Permanently Incapacitated.

Finding his party fractured by the murder of John Baxter with six hundred miles of the Nullarbor Plain still to cross, Eyre wrote: 'The horrors of my situation glared upon me in such startling reality, as for an instant almost to paralyse the mind.' (*Journals of Expeditions of Discovery into Central Australia and Overland from Adelaide to King George's Sound.* T. and W. Boone, 1845, Vol 2, Chapter 1). Nullarbor explorer and first WA Premier Sir John Forrest declared in 1917 that 'East and West are indissolubly joined together by bands of steel … A great triumph of civilisation has come in my day.' (*Adelaide Advertiser*, 'The East-West Railway: Sir John Forrest's Triumph', 18 October 1917). Douglas (later Sir Douglas) Nicholls recalled 'I saw my people on the Nullarbor Plain when I was crossing by train, running to and fro by the carriages, begging, crying "Gibbit, gibbit". They seized pieces of apple peel, scraps of bread that were thrown out the windows and doors. I can never forget it.' ('"White people must think black": Aboriginal spokesman's eloquent plea for his people', *Sun* [Melbourne] November 1940). The 'Big V' is the colloquial name for the Victorian State AFL/VFL team. Journalist and poet Victor Courtney calls Daisy Bates 'the black man's friend' in *Perth—And All This! A Story About a City* (Halstead Press, 1962: 174).

Department of Someones
JobSeeker, formerly Newstart, is the Australian unemployment benefit, predicated on 'mutual obligation', which can compel the recipient to attend interviews, complete team projects or training, or repay overclaimed amounts (mis)determined by algorithm, aka 'robodebt'.

You Yangs and Diving Boards
The You Yangs are granite peaks just north of Geelong, visible behind the diving boards at Corio Bay.

Translated Cranes
Changchung optimistically means 'long Spring'. Its northern latitude means Springs of less than a month, diminished further by human activity.

Earthly Delights
Corresponds with Hieronymous Bosch's famed triptych *Garden of Earthly Delights* (c.1515). Southern Rights were so named as they floated when harpooned, making them the 'right' whale to hunt. Lucas North's 'hologram' line is all I recall of a short story he read to me at UWA. His younger brother Marcus played cricket for Australia.

Reporting the World: John Pilger Exhibition
Journalist John Pilger curated this exhibition of international black and white photography. The cited words are Pilger's, the photographer Eric Piper. (*Reporting the World: John Pilger's Eyewitness Photographers*. 21 Publishing, 2001: 19, 25).

At the Non-Existent Statue of a Speared Arthur Phillip
'Seven miles from Sydney and a thousand miles from care' is a local slogan inscribed at Manly Wharf near brickwork featuring pictures of Bennelong and sealife with Indigenous names. *Galgalla* is one Sydney-area Aboriginal name for smallpox, recorded by Judge Advocate David Collins in *An Account of the English Colony of New South Wales* (1798). By sheer luck, Governor Phillip happened to be missing the

very same tooth that was knocked out in a local Aboriginal initiation ritual, signifying knowledge and status (see episode one of *The First Australians* for more details). The Australian Institute of Police Management (AIPM), which trains federal, local and international police, is located nearby at Collins Beach.

Ultraviolet Dusk Before a Storm

In Plato's *Republic*, Socrates refuses to describe the Form of the Good, but nominates the sun as the Child of the Good.

Cottesloe Nights

Cottesloe is the southern portion of the traditional land of the Mooro people, a significant Whadjuk Noongar group of the Perth area. South of the Cottesloe Groyne are the surf breaks known as The Cove and Seconds; further south is where Willem De Vlamingh anchored in 1696. To the north lies Swanbourne Nude Beach (beside Campbell Barracks, home of SAS soldiers) and Floreat. The megamouth shark (*megachasma pelagios*) is a deepwater shark first discovered in 1976. Wadjemup is the Noongar name for Rottnest Island, used to isolate and execute Aboriginal prisoners prior to WWII, thereafter a tourist hotspot. Peter's Pool is a lagoon at the north end of Cottesloe beach. Lake Claremont/Galbamaanup skirts the defunct drive-in near the former site of Swanbourne Senior High School. From the 1930s to the 1950s, Noongar families were evicted from the local area as part of a push for 'redevelopment'. The Swanway Crescent memorial to the evicted families is a recent initiative of the Town of Claremont. 'Derros': slang for 'derelicts', attributable to any ne'er-do-well. 'Vegie maths' was an SSHS student name for the weakest maths level, ie. maths for 'vegetables'.

Acknowledgements

This collection would not have been possible without the support of David Musgrave and the team at Puncher and Wattman, the Australia Council, Macquarie University (particularly my Head of Discipline Hsu-Ming Teo) and my many friends and mentors in the Perth, Sydney, Melbourne and Canberra poetry worlds—Mal McKimmie, Mark Reid, Philip Salom, Jennifer Harrison, David Malouf, Robert Adamson, Juno Gemes, Judith Beveridge, Marcelle Freiman, Lachlan Brown, Desmonda Kearney, Brian Hawkins, Paul Magee, Jakob Ziguras, Luke Fischer and Dalia Nassar. My heartfelt thanks to my wondrous partner Erin and the Claringbold family and to my parents Gary and Barbara and the Davidson clan for their love and support. Thanks to Mum and an unknown traveller for the cover photos.

The following works have informed some of the poems: Larissa Behrendt (dir.), *Maralinga Tjarutja* (Blackfella Films, 2020); David Burke, *Road Through the Wilderness: The Story of the Transcontinental Railway, the First Great Work of Australia's Federation* (UNSW Press, 1991); Inga Clendinnen, *Dancing with Strangers: Europeans and Australians at First Contact* (Text, 2003); Curtin University and City of Stirling in consultation with Professor Len Collard, *Mooro Nyungar Katitjin Bidi (Mooro People's Knowledge Trail)* (City of Stirling, 2013); A.G. Evans, *C.Y. O'Connor: His Life and Legacy* (UWA Publishing, 2001); Edward John Eyre, *Journals of Expeditions of Discovery into Central Australia and Overland from Adelaide to King George's Sound* (T. and W. Boone, 1845); friendsoflakeclaremont.org; Ruth Marchant James, *A Heritage of Pines: A History of the Town of Cottesloe, Western Australia* (Town of Cottesloe, 1992); Rachel Perkins and Beck Cole (dirs.), *The First Australians, Episode 1: They Have Come to Stay* (Blackfella Films, 2008).

Four Oceans was written in Whadjuk Noongar, Wurundjeri, Gundijmara, Kirrae Wurrong, Darug, Gadigal, Guringai and Gayamaygal Country, Australia, and in the Nations crossed by the Trans-Australian Railway.

About the Author

Toby Davidson was born in Perth in 1977 and grew up in the beachside suburb of Cottesloe. In 2002 he moved to Sydney, then to Melbourne and Warrnambool, where he completed a PhD at Deakin University. He is presently a senior lecturer at Macquarie University, editor of Francis Webb's *Collected Poems* and author of two scholarly studies, *Christian Mysticism and Australian Poetry* and *Good for the Soul: John Curtin's Life with Poetry*. His first collection, *Beast Language* (free at https://fiveislandspress.com/featured-books/beast-language), was anthologised in *Contemporary Australian Poetry*, *The Fremantle Press Anthology of Western Australian Poetry*, *The Weekly Poem* and *Best Australian Poems*.

Poems in this collection have previously appeared in *Antipodes*, *Australian Poetry Collaboration*, *Cordite*, *The Disappearing* (Red Room Company), *The Hunger* (eds. Michelle Seminara and Robbie Coburn), *Mascara*, *Meniscus*, *Messages from the Embers* (eds. Denise O'Hagan and Julia Kaylock), *Plumwood Mountain*, *Rabbit*, *Truth or Beauty: Biographical Poetry* (eds. Anna Jackson, Helen Rickerby, Angelina Sbroma), *Verity LA* and *Westerly*.